BROADWAY
TRIVIA

Be A Broadway Star LLC, 2019

Be A Broadway Star
1501 Broadway, Suite 1304
New York, NY 10036
(212) 874-5348
play@beabroadwaystar.com

BROADWAY
TRIVIA

TABLE OF CONTENTS

Chapter One: Broadway Theaters..5

Chapter Two: History of the Great White Way..................14

Chapter Three: Name That Tune 22

Chapter Four: Tony Award Trivia.....................................31

Chapter Five: Writers & Composers 39

Chapter Six: Broadway's Brightest Stars 47

Chapter Seven: Famous Flops 55

Chapter Eight: Holiday Hits 63

Chapter Nine: National Tours..71

Answer Key 78

CHAPTER ONE

Broadway Theaters

Think you're an expert on Broadway Theaters? Let's find out!

EASY:

1. What Olivier winner was featured in Matilda in 2013 in the Shubert Theater?

    A. Lesli Margherita

    B. Cassie Silva

    C. Lauren Ward

    D. Jennifer Bowles

2. In 1993, what company began restructuring the New Amsterdam Theater?

    A. FOX

    B. Comcast

    C. Disney

    D. CBS

3. What theatre is named in honor of a famed actor whose brother assassinated the sixteenth president of the United States?

A. Hudson Theater

B. Cort Theater

C. Booth Theater

D. Hayes Theater

4. What theater is the longest running show in Broadway history still playing at?

    A. Majestic

    B. Imperial

    C. Lyric

    D. Palace

5. The Marquis Theater debuted this show about a three-time Grammy award-winning
Cuban-American artist and her husband in 2015.

    A. *In The Heights*

    B. *On Your Feet*

    C. *Once*

    D. *If/Then*

6. The biggest theater on Broadway, seating 1,935.

    A. Gershwin Theater

    B. Belasco Theater

    C. Winter Garden Theater

    D. Eugene O'Neill Theater

7. As of 2018, *Chicago* has been playing at this theater since 2003.

    A. Gershwin Theater

    B. Broadhurst Theater

    C. Minskoff Theater

    D. Ambassador Theater

8. This theater bore the names Forrest & Coronet before being given the name it bears today.

    A. Eugene O'Neill Theater

    B. Sondheim Theater

    C. Richard Rodgers Theater

    D. Palace Theater

9. This production played at the 46th street Theater, St. James Theater and the Majestic Theater during its three year run.

    A. *Hair*

    B. *Evita*

    C. *1776*

    D. *Bye Bye Birdie*

10. What was the first theater to be granted landmark status in 1974?

    A. New Amsterdam Theater

    B. Lyceum Theater

    C. Majestic Theater

    D. Booth Theater

MEDIUM:

1. *Wake Up and Dream* opened at this theater in 1929. The theater has since been renamed to the American Airlines Theater.
- **A.** Selwyn Theater
- **B.** Majestic Theater
- **C.** Belasco Theater
- **D.** Broadway Theater

2. As of 2018, the Shubert organization owns how many Broadway theaters?
- **A.** 14
- **B.** 15
- **C.** 17
- **D.** 20

3. What Broadway theater has *West Side Story* not played in?
- **A.** Winter Garden Theater
- **B.** Marquis Theater
- **C.** Minskoff Theater
- **D.** Palace Theater

4. The silent film actress, Olive Thomas, is said to haunt the New Amsterdam Theater and she is often seen...
- **A.** With a yellow purse
- **B.** In her follies outfit

C. Carrying a blue bottle

D. Smoking a cigarette

5. Herbert J. Krapp was an architect on all of the following theaters except:

    A. Neil Simon Theater

    B. New Amsterdam Theater

    C. Brooks Atkinson Theater

    D. Richard Rodgers Theater

6. At its opening, it was the only Broadway theater to be owned outright without a mortgage.

    A. Palace Theater

    B. Stephen Sondheim Theater

    C. Nederlander Theater

    D. Al Hirschfeld Theater

7. This theater was constructed in 1917-18 and was given landmark status in 1987.

    A. Gerald Schoenfeld Theater

    B. Neil Simon Theater

    C. John Golden Theater

    D. Minskoff Theater

8. As of 2018, *Once* holds the box office record at this theater, grossing $1,477,598 over nine performances.

    A. Bernard B. Jacobs Theater

B. Shubert Theater

C. New Amsterdam Theater

D. Winter Garden Theater

9. As of 2018 all of the following are names of theaters in both the West End and Broadway except:

    A. Ambassador

    B. Majestic

    C. Lyceum

    D. Palace

10. *A Chorus Line* used this theater as the exterior for the 1985 film.

    A. Golden Theater

    B. Broadhurst Theater

    C. Brooks Atkinson Theater

    D. Vivian Beaumont Theater

HARD:

1. Which actress made a time capsule and buried it under the carpeting in one of the Shubert's rooms?

    A. Heather Tepe

    B. Carol Channing

    C. Ali Ewoldt

    D. Idina Menzel

2. Who were the designers of the New Amsterdam Theater in 1903?

    A. John Eberson

    B. Mark Fischer

    C. Henry Herts and Hugh Tallant

    D. G Albert Lansbergh

3. What theater had a 10-room apartment built into the theater for the person the theater was named after?

    A. Belasco

    B. Sondheim

    C. Neil Simon

    D. August Wilson

4. Which theater house is the only accredited training conservatory associated with a Broadway theater?

    A. Gershwin

    B. Richard Rodgers

    C. Circle in the Square

    D. Minskoff

5. Which theater holds the record for housing the most number of shows that have won either the Best Play or Best Musical Tony Award: nine musicals and two plays?

    A. Stephen Sondheim

    B. Nederlander

C. St. James

D. Richard Rodgers

6. What Broadway producer, who owned the Hudson and Hackett Theater, died in the sinking of the Titanic?

    A. Florenz Ziegfeld

    B. Henry B. Harris

    C. David Merrick

    D. Fred Ebb

7. The Vivian Beaumont Theater opened in 1965 with a revival of this play...

    A. *Danton's Death*

    B. *Kiss Me, Kate*

    C. *Oklahoma*

    D. *South Pacific*

8. What theater is home to the ghost of a vaudeville actor that is seen walking a tightrope from the house left box to the mezzanine?

    A. Belasco Theater

    B. New Amsterdam Theater

    C. Palace Theater

    D. Majestic Theater

9. Anna Deavere Smith debuted her one woman play here in 1994 where it ran for 72 performances.

A. Sondheim Theater

B. Richard Rodgers Theater

C. Minskoff Theater

D. Cort Theater

11. *A Chorus Line* used this theater as the exterior for the 1985 film.

A. Golden Theater

B. Broadhurst Theater

C. Brooks Atkinson Theater

D. Vivian Beaumont Theater

CHAPTER TWO

History of the Great White Way

Here's some general Broadway Trivia to test your knowledge!

EASY:

1. As of 2018, this individual has 21 Tony awards, more than anyone else.
- **A.** Hal Prince
- **B.** Andrew Lloyd-Webber
- **C.** Audra McDonald
- **D.** Richard Rodgers

2. As of 2018, this is the longest running revival on Broadway.
- **A.** *The Lion King*
- **B.** *Les Miserables*
- **C.** *Chicago*
- **D.** *The Sound of Music*

3. Why is Broadway often called the Great White Way?

A. There were predominately white actors

B. The white lights from the theater marquis

C. The streets were originally paved with white cement

D. The theaters used to be mainly along White St.

4. What was seen as the biggest threat to live theatre in the 1920's?

A. Sports Games

B. Motion Pictures

C. Radio

D. Commercial Flights

5. How many seats does a theatre need to be considered a Broadway Theater?

A. 300

B. 450

C. 500

D. 650

6. How long did Rodgers and Hammerstein's first collaboration, *Oklahoma*, run for?

A. Less than 1,500 performances

B. Between 1,500 and 2,000 performances

C. Between 2,000 and 2,500 performances

D. More than 2,500 performances

7. What years are commonly considered as Broadway's Golden Age?

A. 1912-1925

B. 1943-1959

C. 1971-1984

D. 1991-2004

8. What was the first Broadway show to play at the White House?

   A. *Chorus Line*

   B. *West Side Story*

   C. *1776*

   D. *Camelot*

9. What was the first Broadway show to transfer from Off-Broadway?

   A. *Rent*

   B. *Spring Awakening*

   C. *Hair*

   D. *West Side Story*

10. What title character of a Shakespeare play is considered bad luck to say in a theater?

   A. *Hamlet*

   B. *King Henry IV*

   C. *Macbeth*

   D. *Othello*

MEDIUM:

1. As of 2018 how many Broadway theatres are there?
   - **A.** 37
   - **B.** 41
   - **C.** 46
   - **D.** 52

2. Often considered the first musical, *The Black Crook* was how many hours long?
   - **A.** 2.5 Hours
   - **B.** 4 Hours
   - **C.** 5.5 Hours
   - **D.** 7 Hours

3. *Irene* passed the previous record for longest running musical in 1919. What show did *Irene* dethrone?
   - **A.** *42nd Street*
   - **B.** *A Trip to Chinatown*
   - **C.** *Old Town*
   - **D.** *Bright Eyes*

4. The name of America's oldest professional theatrical organization whose members include Oscar Hammerstein II, Irving Berlin, Fred Astaire and Cecil B. Demille.
   - **A.** The Lambs
   - **B.** American Theatre Wing
   - **C.** Manhattan Theatre Club

D. Gold Club

5. What Broadway show didn't have an Off-Broadway run before transferring to Broadway?
   A. *Rent*
   B. *Spring Awakening*
   C. *Waitress*
   D. *Hamilton*

6. How old was Irving Berlin when he died in 1989?
   A. 87
   B. 92
   C. 98
   D. 101

7. What part did Julie Andrew make her Broadway debut in?
   A. Polly Browne
   B. Eliza Doolittle
   C. Princess Badroulbadour
   D. Cinderella

8. Which two composers collaborated on the 1927 musical *Show Boat*?
   A. Kern & Hammerstein
   B. Berlin & Porter
   C. Rodgers & Hart
   D. Gershwin & Bernstein

9. Where was the theater district mainly located before it moved to midtown in the mid nineteenth-century?
  A. Upper East Side
  B. Downtown Manhattan
  C. Harlem
  D. Brooklyn

10. What did not contribute to larger audiences coming to the theater district in the early twentieth century?
  A. New York's Rapid Transit system was improved
  B. More street lighting made it safer to be out at night.
  C. Family shows such as Robin Hood and El Captain were shown
  D. Nine new theatres were built

HARD:

1. What show has the longest time without a note of music being played or sung for nearly thirty minutes?
  A. *1776*
  B. *Dear Evan Hansen*
  C. *Bye Bye Birdie*
  D. *The Band's Visit*

2. What was the first Broadway show to reach 1,000 performances?
  A. *3 Showers*

B. *Madame Pompadour*

C. *Blue Eyes*

D. *Lightnin'*

3. What year did the Tony's not present awards in Lead Actor in a Musical, Lead Actress in a Musical and Best Choreography?
   A. 1957
   B. 1968
   C. 1972
   D. 1985

4. What show had actors performing from the house after the WPA shut down production four days before opening?
   A. *The Cradle Will Rock*
   B. *Little By Little*
   C. *Flora the Red Menace*
   D. *A Minister's Wife*

5. What show did Irving Berlin write and tour with during World War II?
   A. *Miss Liberty*
   B. *George Washington Jr*
   C. *Of Thee I sing*
   D. *This is the Army*

6. When was the first Vaudeville theater opened in New York?
   A. 1845
   B. 1862
   C. 1881

D. 1898

7. When was Actors Equity, a labor union representing live theatrical performers, founded?
   A. April 7th, 1909
   B. May 26th, 1913
   C. September 13th, 1916
   D. July 22nd, 1919

8. Who wears the Gypsy Robe on the opening night of a Broadway Musical?
   A. The Lead actor in the show
   B. Cast members vote for who wears it
   C. The chorus member with the most Broadway credits
   D. It is passed around the entire cast and crew

9. What is the light that is left on in Broadway theaters when they are empty called?
   A. Ghost Light
   B. Safety Lamp
   C. Stage Light
   D. Curtain Lamp

10. What are you not supposed to do in a theater?
   A. Snap your fingers
   B. Clap before final curtain
   C. Stomp your feet
   D. Whistle

CHAPTER THREE

Name That Tune

How well do you know your show tunes?

EASY:

1. Who wrote the lyric, "Look around, look around at how lucky we are to be alive right now! History is happening in Manhattan and we just happen to be in the greatest city in the world"?
   A. Ryan Scott Oliver
   B. Lin-Manuel Miranda
   C. Oscar Hammerstein II
   D. Stephen Sondheim

2. Finish this lyric from *Wicked*, "I'll teach you the proper poise when you talk to boys / Little ways to flirt and flounce, ooh! / I'll Show you what shoes to wear, how to ____"
   A. Fix your hair
   B. Get good grades
   C. Pick locks
   D. Pick out clothes

3. What show is the song "96,000" from?

    A. *Urinetown*

    B. *The 25th Annual Putnam County Spelling Bee*

    C. *In The Heights*

    D. *Producers*

4. What song does the lyric "The world, for once, in perfect harmony / With all its living things" come from?

    A. "Can You Feel the Love Tonight"

    B. "Without Love"

    C. "Joseph's Dreams"

    D. "Ever After"

5. What show is the song "Before the Parade Passes By" from?

    A. *Carousel*

    B. *Parade*

    C. *Hello, Dolly!*

    D. *Oklahoma*

6. What year was the cast album for *Dear Evan Hansen* released?

    A. 2015

    B. 2016

    C. 2017

    D. 2018

7. Who wrote the lyric, "You alone can make the song take flight / help me make the music of the night"?

    A. Cole Porter

    B. Andrew Lloyd Webber

    C. Rodgers and Hammerstein

D. Alan Menken

8. Finish this lyric from *West Side Story*, "I feel stunning / And entrancing / Feel like running and dancing for joy / For I'm loved / By a pretty _____ "
   A. Fabulous boy
   B. Wonderful boy
   C. Gorgeous boy
   D. Intelligent boy

9. What show does the lyric "Friday night and the lights are low / Looking out for a place to go / Where they play the right music / Getting in the swing / You come to look for a king" come from?
   A. *The Wild Party*
   B. *Honeymoon in Vegas*
   C. *Summer: The Donna Summer Musical*
   D. *Mamma Mia!*

10. What lyric is not from Cole Porter's musical *Anything Goes*?
    A. "Once I was headed for hell: / But when I got to Satan's door / I heard you blowin' on your horn once more, So I said, 'Satan, Farewell!'"
    B. "Where is the life that late I led? / Where is it now? Totally dead."
    C. "When other friendships have ceased to jell / ours will still be swell!"
    D. "In olden days, a glimpse of stocking was looked on as something shocking"

MEDIUM:

1. What show is the song "The Pitiful Children" from?

    A. *13*

    B. *Children of Eden*

    C. *Calvin Berger*

    D. *Be More Chill*

2. Who wrote the lyric, "It's addictive the minute you let yourself think / The things that I say just might matter to someone"?

    A. Sara Bareilles

    B. Tim Rice

    C. Elton John

    D. Stephen Schwartz

3. The Rodgers and Hammerstein lyrics "A blue eyed kid / I liked her a lot / We got engaged / both families were glad" appear in which R & H show?

    A. *Carousel*

    B. *Oklahoma*

    C. *South Pacific*

    D. *The Sound of Music*

4. What song is not from Gershwin's show *Me and My Girl*?

    A. "Once You Lose your Heart"

    B. "If Only You Had cared for Me"

    C. "An English Gentleman"

    D. "I'll Hold Your Hand"

5. Which of these lyrics would not be found in *Into The Woods*?
- **A.** "A ball and that's not all! / The Prince is giving a ball"
- **B.** "Though it's fearful / Though it's deep, through it's dark / And though you may lose the path"
- **C.** "Can't we just pursue our lives / with our children and our wives / 'Till that happy day arrives"
- **D.** "When the one thing you want / Is the only thing out of your reach"

6. What year was the music from *Rent* first performed on Broadway?
- **A.** 1996
- **B.** 1997
- **C.** 1998
- **D.** 1999

7. What musical does not have a song titled "Beautiful" in it?
- **A.** *Heathers*
- **B.** *Ordinary Days*
- **C.** *Sunday In The Park With George*
- **D.** *Evita*

8. What song does the lyric "I saw this light / And it was neat" come from?
- **A.** "I'm Not That Smart"
- **B.** "Woe is Me"
- **C.** "Heave Away"
- **D.** "On the Streets of Dublin"

9. Who wrote the lyrics, "Sunrise, sunset / Swiftly fly the years / One season following another / Laden with happiness and tears" that made their Broadway debut in 1964?

    A. David Shire

    B. Andrew Lippa

    C. Richard Thomas

    D. Sheldon Harnick

10. Finish this lyric from *The Wild Party*, "Let's raise the roof / Let's make a scene / Let's hope the gods of love / Will shine above / And show the way. / _____"

    A. Let's call the shots

    B. Just hold me tight

    C. Let's roll the dice

    D. Just close your eyes

HARD:

1. Finish the lyric from *A Little Night Music*, "It's a rip in the bustle and a rustle in the hay / And I'll _____"

    A. Pitch the quick fantastic

    B. Foot the highland fancy

    C. Trip the light fandango

    D. Sigh the whole night through

2. Who is credited with writing the lyrics to the song "I Draw the Line" in 1990?

    A. Fred Ebb

B. Cy Coleman

C. John Kander

D. George Gershwin

3. Finish this lyric from *Company*, "It's the little things you do together / Do together / Do together / That make perfect relationships / The hobbies you pursue together / _____"

    A. Looks you misconstrue together

    B. Savings you accrue together

    C. Children you destroy together

    D. Neighbors you annoy together

4. What song is from *Bare: A Pop Opera*?

    A. "Epic"

    B. "Memories of You"

    C. "Queen Mab"

    D. "If We Kissed"

5. Finish this lyric from *The Last Five Years*, "Will you share your life with me / For the next ten minutes? / For the next ten minutes: / _____"

    A. 'Till the morning comes

    B. 'Till the world explodes

    C. As the time ticks by

    D. We can handle that

6. In what musical do the lyrics, "When a girl asks a guy to hang out / what could that be about / you tell me!" appear in?

    A. *Avenue Q*

B. *Calvin Berger*

C. *Be More Chill*

D. *The Lightning Thief: The Percy Jackson Musical*

7. What song is not from the musical *Bridges of Madison County*?

    A. "Falling Into You"

    B. "Temporarily Lost"

    C. "The Real World"

    D. "Look At Her"

8. What year is the *A Man of No Importance* Off-Broadway Cast recording from?

    A. 1997

    B. 2000

    C. 2002

    D. 2005

9. What character sings the lyrics "You don't believer in anything, not even yourself / You don't even believer you're a woman"?

    A. Starbuck

    B. Porgy

    C. Bill

    D. Eliza

10. What song does the lyric "Hello to married men I've known, I'll soon have a wife an' leave yours alone" come from?

    A. "Finian's Rainbow"

    B. "Allegro"

C. "Camelot"

D. "Brigadoon"

CHAPTER FOUR

Tony Award Trivia

How much do you know about "Broadway's Biggest Night"?

EASY:

1. Who was the first female to win Best Director of a Musical?
> **A.** Leigh Silverman
> **B.** Rebecca Taichman
> **C.** Julie Taymor
> **D.** Diane Paulus

2. As of 2018, what show holds the record for the most Tony nominations?
> **A.** *The Producers*
> **B.** *Wicked*
> **C.** *Hamilton*
> **D.** *West Side Story*

3. As of 2018, which actress holds the record for winning the most Tony Awards, not including honorary awards?

A. Sutton Foster
B. Patti Lupone
C. Audra McDonald
D. Julie Harris

4. For what show did Sutton Foster win her first Tony Award?
   A. *The Drowsy Chaperone*
   B. *Thoroughly Modern Millie*
   C. *Little Women*
   D. *Anything Goes*

5. What show did Laura Benanti win a Tony Award for Best Featured Actress?
   A. *Gypsy*
   B. *Nine*
   C. *Women on the Verge of a Nervous Breakdown*
   D. *Into the Woods*

6. For what show did Julie Andrews win her first Tony Award?
   A. *Cinderella*
   B. *My Fair Lady*
   C. *Victor/Victoria*
   D. *Camelot*

7. What Stephen Sondheim show did not win a Tony for Best New Musical?
   A. *A Funny Thing Happened on the Way to the Forum*
   B. *Company*
   C. *Into the Woods*

D. *A Little Night Music*

8. In 2004, what show won Best Musical, beating out *Wicked*?
   A. *Spamalot*
   B. *The 25th Annual Putnam County Spelling Bee*
   C. *Avenue Q*
   D. *Hairspray*

9. Who are the Tony Awards named after?
   A. Tony Bennet
   B. Tony Danza
   C. Antoinette Perry
   D. Antonia Bennet

10. Who won the Tony for Best Musical in 2017?
   A. *Dear Evan Hansen*
   B. *Hamilton*
   C. *The Band's Visit*
   D. *Come From Away*

MEDIUM:

1. What show was nominated for 12 Tony Awards and didn't win any in 2011?
   A. *Hairspray*
   B. *The Music Man*
   C. *Pacific Overtures*

D. *Scottsboro Boys*

2. Who has not hosted three consecutive Tony Awards?
>   **A.** Hugh Jackman
>   **B.** Bud Collyer
>   **C.** Angela Lansbury
>   **D.** Nathan Lane

3. Who did not receive a Tony nomination for their performance in *Next to Normal*?
>   **A.** Alice Ripley
>   **B.** J. Robert Spencer
>   **C.** Jennifer Damiano
>   **D.** Aaron Tveit

4. As of 2018, who is the oldest person to win a Tony Award?
>   **A.** Cicely Tyson
>   **B.** Angela Lansbury
>   **C.** Frank Langella
>   **D.** Roy Dotrice

5. For what show did Kristin Chenoweth not receive a Tony Nomination for?
>   **A.** *You're a Good Man, Charlie Brown*
>   **B.** *Wicked*
>   **C.** *The Apple Tree*
>   **D.** *On the Twentieth Century*

6. What was the first show to win Best Musical at the Tony Awards in 1949?

    A. *South Pacific*

    B. *Guys and Dolls*

    C. *Kiss Me, Kate*

    D. *The King and I*

7. What was the first show to win Best Play at the Tony Awards in 1948?

    A. *Mister Roberts*

    B. *Death of a Salesman*

    C. *The Crucible*

    D. *The Diary of Anne Frank*

8. What year did the Tony Awards officially start?

    A. 1946

    B. 1947

    C. 1948

    D. 1949

9. As of 2018, what show holds the record for the most Tony Awards received by a single production?

    A. *Hamilton*

    B. *Angels in America*

    C. *Hello, Dolly!*

    D. *The Producers*

10. Who won the Tony for Best Musical at the 13th Tony Awards?

> **A.** *Redhead*
> **B.** *Flower Drum Song*
> **C.** *La Plume de Ma Tante*
> **D.** *West Side Story*

HARD:

1. What show's publicity resulted in advance sales of 3.5 million dollars and ran for three years (873 performances) even though it was passed over for a Best Musical nomination in 1961?

> **A.** *Camelot*
> **B.** *Cinderella*
> **C.** *Gigi*
> **D.** *My Fair Lady*

2. What actress turned down her nomination for Best Actress because she felt the show that she was in had been "egregiously overlooked" when it did not receive any other nominations in 1996?

> **A.** Carol Burnett
> **B.** Julie Andrews
> **C.** Zoe Caldwell
> **D.** Donna Murphy

3. As of 2018, who is the youngest person to win a Tony Award?

> **A.** Anna Kendrick

B. Audrey Hepburn

C. Daisy Eagan

D. Frankie Michaels

4. Who was the host at the first Tony Awards?

    A. Bert Lytell

    B. Harry Hershfield

    C. James Sauter

    D. Brock Pemberton

5. Where were the first seven Tony Awards held?

    A. Plaza Hotel

    B. Hotel Astor

    C. Waldorf Astoria, New York

    D. Hotel America

6. In 1960, *The Sound of Music* tied for Best Musical with what other show?

    A. *Fiorello!*

    B. *Gypsy*

    C. *Once Upon A Mattress*

    D. *Flower Drum Song*

7. What year did Stephen Sondheim win his first Tony Award for Best Musical?

    A. 1963

    B. 1967

    C. 1971

    D. 1973

8. What year were all of the nominated shows for Best Musicals previously films?

    A. 2010

    B. 2012

    C. 2014

    D. 2015

9. As of 2017, what year did the Tony awards have the most U.S. viewers (20 million)?

    A. 1974

    B. 1997

    C. 1999

    D. 2016

10. As of 2017, what is the most honored play in Tony history winning Best Play in 1949 and Best Revival of a Play in 1984, 1999, and 2012?

    A. *Hamlet*

    B. *Death of a Salesman*

    C. *Long Day's Journey Into Night*

    D. *Angels in America*

CHAPTER FIVE
Writers and Composers

Do you know who wrote your favorite show tunes? Let's find out!

EASY:

1. What show is the Rodgers and Hart jazz standard, "Bewitched, Bothered, and Bewildered" from?
   A. *Pal Joey*
   B. *I Married an Angel*
   C. *The Boys from Syracuse*
   D. *The Girl Friend*

2. What was Rodgers and Hammerstein's last work together?
   A. *Flower Drum Song*
   B. *The Sound of Music*
   C. *The King and I*
   D. *Cinderella*

3. Which musical did Alan Menken not write music for?
   A. *Aladdin*

B. *The Little Mermaid*

C. *The Lion King*

D. *Beauty and the Beast*

4. What singer/songwriter wrote the lyrics and music for *Waitress*?

    A. Ingrid Michaelson

    B. Joni Mitchell

    C. Sara Bareilles

    D. Regina Spektor

5. Who did not write music for *SpongeBob SquarePants, the Broadway Musical*?

    A. The Flaming Lips

    B. John Legend

    C. Panic! At the Disco

    D. Fall Out Boy

6. What show did not have one of its composers or writers also act in it on Broadway?

    A. *Kinky Boots*

    B. *Waitress*

    C. *In the Heights*

    D. *Hedwig and the Angry Inch*

7. This George Gershwin musical has been revived seven times, more than any other musical.

    A. *Strike Up the Band*

    B. *Porgy & Bess*

C. *Rosalie*

D. *Let 'Em Eat Cake*

8. Which musical pair have not collaborated together?

    A. Pasek & Paul

    B. Schonberg & Boublil

    C. Rodgers & Sondheim

    D. Minchin & Miranda

9. What Broadway composer mentored Stephen Sondheim when he was young?

    A. Oscar Hammerstein

    B. Charles Strouse

    C. Cole Porter

    D. Richard Rodgers

10. What show had the first all-female writing team to win a Tony?

    A. *Fun Home*

    B. *Violet*

    C. *Ragtime*

    D. *Little Women*

MEDIUM:

1. What Frank Loesser show won the 1962 Pulitzer Prize for Drama?

    A. *Guys and Dolls*

    B. *The Most Happy Fella*

C. *Greenwillow*

D. *How to Succeed in Business Without Really Trying*

2. Which of these songs were not written by Lorenz Hart?
   A. "My Funny Valentine"
   B. "I Could Write A Book"
   C. "If I Loved You"
   D. "Falling in Love with Love"

3. What was Andrew Lloyd Webber and Tim Rice's first collaboration?
   A. *The Likes of Us*
   B. *Jesus Christ Superstar*
   C. *Joseph and the Amazing Technicolor Dreamcoat*
   D. *Evita*

4. Other than *Mamma Mia!* what musical did members of the Swedish band ABBA, Björn Ulvaeus and Benny Andersson, work on?
   A. *The Secret Garden*
   B. *Chess*
   C. *Wonderland*
   D. *Billy Elliot*

5. Which of these shows did Betty Comden not win a Tony for?
   A. *The Will Rogers Follies*
   B. *Singin' in the Rain*
   C. *On the Twentieth Century*
   D. *Hallelujah, Baby!*

6. Kander & Ebb's first collaboration was on an unproduced musical called:

    A. *Zorba*

    B. *Bedazzled*

    C. *Curtains*

    D. *Golden Gate*

7. Which composer is not a graduate of Wesleyan University?

    A. Stephen Trask

    B. Jeanine Tesori

    C. Lin-Manuel Miranda

    D. Joss Whedon

8. Composers Stephen Sondheim, Max Richter, Angelo Badalamenti and Andrew Lloyd Webber all have their birthdays on this date

    A. January 6th

    B. March 22nd

    C. July 12th

    D. September 7th

9. What Schoolhouse Rock song has Lynn Ahrens not written?

    A. "The Preamble"

    B. "Interjections!"

    C. "The Shot Heard Round the World"

    D. "Three Ring Government"

10. Jonathan Larson's first staged creative work was co-written with David Glenn Armstrong and was originally called:

    A. *Sacrimmoralinority*

B. *Tick, tick... BOOM*

C. *Superbia*

D. *Rent*

HARD:

1. Which famous writing duo made their professional debut with the song "Any Old Place With You" that was featured in the musical *A Lonely Romeo*?

    A. Rodgers and Hammerstein

    B. Rodgers and Hart

    C. Lerner and Lowe

    D. Sondheim and Lapine

2. Andrew Lloyd Webber was asked to write a song for the Olympics. What year?

    A. 1990

    B. 1992

    C. 1995

    D. 1997

3. Which composer won the Tony award for Best Original Score in 1968 for *Hallelujah, Baby!*?

    A. Harold Arlen

    B. John Farrar

    C. Jule Styne

    D. Sammy Cahn

4. Which of these shows did Ryan Scott Oliver not write?

   A. *Jasper in Deadland*

   B. *35MM: A Musical Exhibition*

   C. *We Foxes*

   D. *Venice*

5. Judy Garland performed a medley of Cole Porter's songs at the

   A. 37th Academy Awards

   B. 18th Tony Awards

   C. 40th Academy Awards

   D. 15th Tony Awards

6. Which movie sequel has Jeanine Tesori not worked on?

   A. *The Little Mermaid: Ariel's Beginning*

   B. *Mulan II*

   C. *The Emperor's New Groove 2: Kronk's New Groove*

   D. *Shrek 2*

7. Which writer or composer did not work on the operetta-style musical, *Rose-Marie*?

   A. Rudolf Friml

   B. Herbert Stothart

   C. Lorenz Hart

   D. Oscar Hammerstein II

8. What year did Leonard Bernstein first conduct the entirety of *West Side Story*?

   A. 1985

   B. 1957

C. 1963

D. 1980

9. What composer wrote a 1962 musical with a book by Mel Brooks and lyrics by Lee Adams?

   A. Charles Strouse

   B. Frank Loesser

   C. Jerry Bock

   D. Alan Jay Lerner

10. Which famous Broadway composer is a fan of tennis and has won trophies in local tournaments?

   A. Stephen Sondheim

   B. Stephen Schwartz

   C. Benj Pasek

   D. Justin Paul

CHAPTER SIX

Broadway's Brightest Stars

Are you a Broadway star super fan? Test your knowledge in this category!

EASY:

1. Which actress played Mama Rose in the original production of *Gypsy*?
   - **A.** Sandra Church
   - **B.** Lane Bradbury
   - **C.** Ethel Merman
   - **D.** Kathryn Albertson

2. As of 2018, this is the youngest person to ever play Eliza Doolittle...
   - **A.** Julie Andrews
   - **B.** Laura Benanti
   - **C.** Kerstin Anderson
   - **D.** Lauren Ambrose

3. This actress originated the role of Eliza Hamilton both on and off-Broadway
   A. Phillipa Soo
   B. Carleigh Bettiol
   C. Alysha Deslorieux
   D. Lexi Lawson

4. Jessie Mueller won a Tony award for Best Actress in a Musical as this character
   A. Julie Jordan
   B. Carole King
   C. Jenna
   D. Melinda Wells

5. Alex Brightman had his Broadway debut in this 2004 Musical
   A. *Chess*
   B. *Little Shop of Horrors*
   C. *Wicked*
   D. *Avenue Q*

6. She is the first person to hit the Billboard Top 10 and win a Tony Award for acting
   A. Idina Menzel
   B. Laura Osnes
   C. Lea Michele
   D. Donna Summer

7. Ramin Karimloo had his Broadway debut as this character
   A. Jean Valjean

B. Gleb

C. The Phantom

D. Barry Hamidi

8. Max Bialystock in *The Producers* was originated by this actor

    A. Brad Oscar

    B. Ray Willis

    C. Zero Mostel

    D. Nathan Lane

9. Jeremy Jordan played Jack in this musical

    A. *Bonnie & Clyde*

    B. *Once*

    C. *Newsies*

    D. *The Mystery of Edwin Drood*

10. She is the most decorated Tony Award winning actress, having won in all four acting categories

    A. Shirley Booth

    B. Audra McDonald

    C. Gwen Verdon

    D. Angela Lansbury

MEDIUM:

1. This show earned Angela Lansbury her fourth Tony Award

    A. *Sweeney Todd*

    B. *Dear World*

C. *Mame*

D. *Deuce*

2. Once referred to as "beady-eyed" in junior high, which Broadway star has been named PEOPLE's 50 Most Beautiful twice?

   A. Taye Diggs

   B. Leslie Odom Jr.

   C. Neil Patrick Harris

   D. Christian Borle

3. Angela Lansbury is the host of the most Tony Awards telecasts having hosted

   A. 3

   B. 5

   C. 7

   D. 9

4. This Actress has played Marty from *Grease*, Maureen from *Rent* and Ursula from *Little Mermaid* on Broadway

   A. Sierra Boggess

   B. Sherie Rene Scott

   C. Susan Wood

   D. Idina Menzel

5. After 52 years in the theater and performance business, which actress finally received her first leading role in a Broadway musical in 2017?

   A. Bernadette Peters

B. Barbra Streisand

C. Bette Midler

D. Christine Ebersole

6. Which actor has played Elder Price in *Book of Mormon* longest with a record of 6 and a half years and 2,500 performances?

    A. Andrew Rannells

    B. Nic Rouleau

    C. Gavin Creel

    D. Gavin Lee

7. Who made their Broadway debut in *Footloose*?

    A. Christian Borle

    B. Dee Hoty

    C. Megan Hilty

    D. Jenn Colella

8. Who replaced Kelli O'Hara in *Nice Work if You Can Get It*?

    A. Judy Kaye

    B. Chilina Kennedy

    C. Jessie Mueller

    D. Abby Mueller

9. How many shows has Cameron Adams performed in?

    A. 10

    B. 12

    C. 30

    D. 31

10. How many times has Jennfier Simard been on Broadway?

    A. 6

    B. 7

    C. 10

    D. 5

HARD:

1. This Broadway actress's car collided with a taxi causing injuries which included the breaking of her left leg in twelve places. After rehabilitation, she returned to the Broadway stage.

    A. Patricia Morison

    B. Chita Rivera

    C. Onna White

    D. Liza Minnelli

2. She was part of the first graduating class of Juilliard's Drama Division.

    A. Patti Ann LuPone

    B. Meryl Streep

    C. Diane Keaton

    D. Bernadette Peters

3. Which actor performed in Sweet Charity with a broken foot?

    A. Shannon Lewis

    B. Kyra Da Costa

    C. Christina Applegate

D. Charlotte d'Amboise

4. How many actors played the Alternate Spiderman in
Spiderman: Turn Off the Dark?
- **A.** 4
- **B.** 3
- **C.** 5
- **D.** 7

5. Name the 4 Actors who played the Alternate Spiderman in
Spiderman: Turn Off the Dark.
- **A.** Jake Epstein, Jason Gotay, Matthew James Thomas, and Andrew Garfield
- **B.** Jake Epstein, Jason Gotay, Matt Caplan, and Matthew Wilkas
- **C.** Jake Epstein, Jason Gotay, Andrew Garfield, and Reeve Carney
- **D.** Jake Epstein, Jason Gotay, Justin Matthew Sargent, and Matthew James Thomas

6. What Disney Channel Star is playing Fiyero in *Wicked* on
Broadway?
- **A.** Dove Cameron
- **B.** Amanda Jane Cooper
- **C.** Kevin Chamberlin
- **D.** Ryan McCartan

7. Which of these actors has never performed on Broadway?
- **A.** Kristen Bell

B. Dax Shepard

C. Josh Gad

D. Maia Nkenge Wilson

8. Which star played Grizabella the Glamour Cat in the most recent revival of *Cats*?

    A. Leona Lewis

    B. Nicole Scherzinger

    C. Mamie Parris

    D. Jennifer Hudson

9. Which former Eponine made her Broadway debut in *Pretty Woman*?

    A. Sierra Boggess

    B. Cassie Levy

    C. Samantha Barks

    D. Amanda Seyfried

10. How many shows has Alex Brightman performed in on Broadway (*Beetlejuice* included)?

    A. 5

    B. 7

    C. 6

    D. 8

CHAPTER SEVEN
Famous Flops

You may know a lot about the biggest Broadway shows, but what about some who weren't quite as successful?

EASY:

1. What composer's 1976 musical only ran for seven performances and thirteen previews?
   - **A.** Leonard Bernstein
   - **B.** Mitch Leigh
   - **C.** Stephen Sondheim
   - **D.** Andrew Lloyd Webber

2. Based on the Stephen King novel, *Carrie* closed after 16 previews and five performances and cost how much?
   - **A.** $4 million
   - **B.** $5 million
   - **C.** $8 million
   - **D.** $10 million

3. What musical comedy starring Michael Feinstein and Dame Edna Everage fighting over a solo headlining role lasted only six weeks?
   A. *All About Me*
   B. *American Idiot*
   C. *Elf - The Musical*
   D. *La Cage aux Folles*

4. Tony nominee Phillipa Soo starred in this Broadway musical about a young French woman who didn't interact much with the world but had a huge imagination
   A. *Natasha, Pierre & The Great Comet of 1812*
   B. *Hamilton*
   C. *The Parisian Woman*
   D. *Amelie*

5. This actor made his Broadway debut as David Van Patten in *American Psycho* before going on to star as Elder Price in *The Book of Mormon*
   A. Paul Owen
   B. Dave Thomas Brown
   C. Jason Hite
   D. Jared Gertner

6. Which theater housed the shortest running Broadway performance?
   A. Cort
   B. Golden
   C. Marquis
   D. New Century Theater

7. Opening night was the same as closing night for *Idol: The Musical*, an American Idol inspired show, in what year?

    A. 2003

    B. 2005

    C. 2007

    D. 2009

8. *Bonnie and Clyde*, starring Jeremy Jordan and Laura Osnes, lasted how long?

    A. 578 performances

    B. 210 performances

    C. 75 performances

    D. 36 performances

9. Which Rodgers and Hammerstein musical ran for 110 performances?

    A. *State Fair*

    B. *Pipe Dream*

    C. *Oklahoma*

    D. *The Sound of Music*

10. Which cult musical starred Charlotte d'Amboise in the titular role?

    A. *Annie*

    B. *Pippin*

    C. *Carrie*

    D. *Sweet Charity*

MEDIUM:

1. Winning a Tony for Best Performance by a Leading Actress in 1954, which Broadway musical closed after only six performances?

 A. *The First Gentleman*
 B. *Carnival in Flanders*
 C. *Slapstick Tragedy*
 D. *All My Sons*

2. Which Leonard Bernstein show ran for only 73 performances?

 A. *West Side Story*
 B. *Pipe Dream*
 C. *Candide*
 D. *State Fair*

3. Which Audrey Hepburn film was revived in 2009 and ran for 140 performances?

 A. *Breakfast at Tiffany's*
 B. *My Fair Lady*
 C. *Roman Holiday*
 D. *Wait Until Dark*

4. Which Tim Curry show ran for 45 performances originally?

 A. *Monty Python's Spamalot*
 B. *The Rocky Horror Picture Show*
 C. *The Pirates of Penzance*
 D. *King Arthur*

5. Which musical starring Rosie O'Donnell played for 100 performances?

    A. *Taboo*

    B. *Grease*

    C. *Tarzan*

    D. *The Rosie O'Donnell Show*

6. Which show with Christopher Plummer only ran for 49 performances?

    A. *The Sound of Music*

    B. *Cyrano*

    C. *All the Money in the World*

    D. *The Last Station*

7. Who starred in *Sweet Bird of Youth*, which ran for 48 performances?

    A. Debra Monk

    B. Christopher Plummer

    C. Ann Margaret

    D. Christopher Walken

8. How many performances of *Redwood Curtain* starring Debra Monk were there?

    A. 40

    B. 39

    C. 30

    D. 20

9. What Al Pacino show ran for 39 performances?

A. *The Godfather*

B. *Does a Tiger Wear a Necktie?*

C. *Scarface*

D. *The Merchant of Venice*

10. Which Andrea Martin show ran for 36 performances?

A. *Pippin*

B. *Noises Off*

C. *My Favorite Year*

D. *Anastasia*

HARD:

1. Which show at the Palace ran for 22 performances?

A. *Liza's at the Palace*

B. *Legally Blonde*

C. *Spongebob Squarepants*

D. *Sunset Boulevard*

2. What show ran for 7 performances only?

A. *Love Never Dies*

B. *Bring Back Birdie*

C. *Slapstick Tragedy*

D. *Rocky*

3. Which play won Best Play and ran for 98 performances?

A. *All My Sons*

B. *Cloud 9*

C. *The Life and Adventures of Nicholas Nickleby*
D. *The Trip to Bountiful*

4. Which revival won Best Play Revival and ran for 31 performances?

A. *All My Sons*
B. *The Life and Adventures of Nicholas Nickleby*
C. *Cloud 9*
D. *The Trip to Bountiful*

5. Which musical running for 280 performances won Best Musical?

A. *Rocky*
B. *The Rocky Horror Picture Show*
C. *Carrie*
D. *Passion*

6. What musical that capitalized at $75 million and lost $60 million closed in 2014?

A. *Spiderman: Turn Off the Dark*
B. *Rocky*
C. *Rocky Horror Picture Show*
D. *Carrie*

7. What show opened at the Brodhurst and closed at a $650,000 loss?

A. *Anastasia*
B. *Kelly*
C. *The Front Page*

D. *Mamma Mia!*

8. Which futuristic musical in the 1960s closed after 7 performances?
   A. *Via Galactica*
   B. *Star Wars: The Empire Strikes Back*
   C. *Star Trek*
   D. *Space Jam*

9. What show at the Cort Theater ran for 19 previews and 61 regular performances?
   A. *Waiting for Godot*
   B. *No Man's Land*
   C. *M. Butterfly*
   D. *The New One*

10. What musical starring Norbert Leo Butz closed after 98 regular performances?
    A. *Big Fish*
    B. *Dirty Rotten Scoundrels*
    C. *Catch Me if You Can*
    D. *The Last Five Years*

CHAPTER EIGHT
Holiday Hits

Featuring questions about shows set on holidays, songs with holidays in them, etc.

EASY:

1. Which holiday show has a score written by the same composer as *Annie Get Your Gun*?
- **A.** *Holiday Inn*
- **B.** *White Christmas*
- **C.** *Promises Promises*
- **D.** *Radio City Christmas Spectacular*

2. What is the name of the show that is set in a famous hotel?
- **A.** *Grand Hotel*
- **B.** *Promises Promises*
- **C.** *Holiday Inn*
- **D.** *A Christmas Story*

3. What is the song in *Promises, Promises* that features Michael Bennett choreography?

A. "I'll Never Fall in Love Again"

B. "Turkey Lurkey Time"

C. "I Say a Little Prayer"

4. Which musical is set in New York and once starred Sarah Jessica Parker in the title role?

    A. *Carrie*

    B. *Annie*

    C. *Cinderella*

    D. *Elf*

5. Which Judy Garland film is a Christmas film because of the song, "Have Yourself a Merry Little Christmas"?

    A. *Easter Parade*

    B. *The Wizard of Oz*

    C. *Meet Me in St. Louis*

    D. *A Star is Born*

6. Which holiday is featured in the show, *Caroline or Change*?

    A. Christmas

    B. Hanukkah or Chanukkah

    C. New Year's

    D. Thanksgiving

7. Which musical marked Zachary Levi's return to the Great White Way?

    A. *First Date*

    B. *She Loves Me*

    C. *Tangled*

D. *Smash*

8. In the musical *Elf*, what is the best way to spread Christmas cheer?
    A. Sprinklejollytwinklejingley
    B. Singing it loud for all to hear
    C. Pouring syrup on spaghetti
    D. Talking to a narwhal

9. Which Jim Carrey character penned the phrase, "Bah Humbug"?
    A. The Grinch- *How the Grinch Stole Christmas*
    B. Count Olaf- *A Series of Unfortunate Events*
    C. Ebenizer Scrooge - *A Christmas Carol*
    D. Horton the Elephant- *Horton Hears a Who!*

10. Which musical starred Gavin Lee at the end of 2018?
    A. *Spongebob Squarepants*
    B. *How the Grinch Stole Christmas*
    C. *Mary Poppins*
    D. *Annie*

MEDIUM:

1. What show set in London wishes Merry Christmas to a British Prime Minister?
    A. *Billy Elliot*
    B. *Mary Poppins*

C. *My Fair Lady*

D. *Mary Poppins Returns*

2. How many holidays does the musical, *Holiday Inn*, cover?
   A. 1
   B. 2
   C. 5
   D. 6

3. Which two holidays does *Rent* cover?
   A. Christmas and New Years Eve
   B. Christmas and Thansgiving
   C. Hanukkah and Christmas
   D. Christmas and Easter

4. What show tells the audience that they "need a little Christmas right this very minute"?
   A. *Hello Dolly*
   B. *Mame*
   C. *White Christmas*
   D. *Annie*

5. Which musical's protagonist wants a BB gun but everyone tells them that they will shoot their eye out?
   A. *A Christmas Story*
   B. *A Christmas Carol*
   C. *Annie*
   D. *White Christmas*

6. Which grumpy character has had an animated short, a live action, and an animated movie?

    A. Ebinezer Scrooge

    B. The Grinch

    C. Squidward Q. Tentacles

    D. Sheldon J. Plankton

7. Which actors originated the roles of Buddy and Santa in *Elf the Musical*?

    A. Sebastian Arcelus and George Wendt

    B. Jordan Gleber and Wayne Knight

    C. Will Ferrell and George Wendt

    D. Jerry Seinfeld and Jason Alexander

8. Who did a one-woman show of grown-up Cindy Lou Who?

    A. Allison Luff

    B. Amy Spanger

    C. Lesli Margherita

    D. Beth Leavel

9. Jimmy Stewart plays the protagonist, George Bailey, in what holiday classic?

    A. *Miracle on 34th St.*

    B. *It's a Wonderful Life*

    C. *Mr. Smith Goes to Washington*

    D. *The Philadelphia Story*

10. From when until when did *Elf* run on Broadway?

    A. November 14, 2010-January 2, 2011

B. November 13, 2010-December 2, 2010

C. November 11,2010-January 2, 2011

D. December 2, 2010-January 2, 2011

HARD:

1. Which holiday show has not been adapted on Broadway?
   A. *Elf*
   B. *Meet Me in St. Louis*
   C. *How the Grinch Stole Christmas*
   D. *Alvin and the Chipmunks*

2. Who originated the role of Mary Lennox in the Broadway production of *Secret Garden?*
   A. Sierra Boggess
   B. Rebecca Luker
   C. Ali Ewoldt
   D. Daisy Eagan

3. Which actress has not played Lily in *Secret Garden*?
   A. Ali Ewoldt
   B. Rebecca Luker
   C. Sierra Boggess
   D. Laura Benanti

4. How many siblings does Esther Smith have in *Meet Me in St. Louis?*
   A. 6

B. 6

C. 4

D. 7

5. Which Tony winner made her Broadway debut in *Meet Me in St. Louis?*

    A. Idina Menzel

    B. Rachel Bay Jones

    C. Liza Minelli

    D. Katrina Lenk

6. Who played Santa in *A Christmas Story* on Broadway?

    A. David Allan Grier

    B. George Wendt

    C. Eddie Korbich

    D. Adam Petty

7. Which Saturday Night Live alum performed in *Promises, Promises*?

    A. Molly Shannon

    B. Maya Rudolph

    C. Tina Fey

    D. Ana Gastyer

8. Which Glee alum was a replacement for Miss Hannigan in the 2012 revival of *Annie*?

    A. Carol Burnett

    B. Jane Lynch

    C. Lea Michele

D. Amber Riley

9. How many orphans are in Miss Hannigan's orphanage in *Annie,* not including Annie?
  A. 6
  B. 5
  C. 7
  D. 8

10. What is the name of the love interest of Esther in *Meet Me in St. Louis?*
  A. Warren Scheffield
  B. Maxwell Scheffield
  C. John Truitt
  D. Alonzo Smith

CHAPTER NINE

National Tours

Featuring questions about shows that have toured, famous casts, and dates of tours.

EASY:

1. Which former Grizabella began her role as matchmaker, Dolly Gallager Levi, on September 30, 2018?
     A. Betty Buckley
     B. Leona Lewis
     C. Mamie Parris
     D. Carol Channing

2. How many languages has *Wicked* been translated into?
     A. 5
     B. 8
     C. 9
     D. 15

3. How many touring companies of *Wicked* were there as of 2018?
     A. 5

B. 6

C. 7

D. 4

4. How many productions of *Come from Away* were open as of 2018?

    A. 5

    B. 6

    C. 3

    D. 8

5. Who played Captain Beverly Bass in *Come from Away* on Broadway, in London, and the National Tour at the same time in 2018?

    A. Jenn Colella, Rachel Tucker, and Becky Gulsvig

    B. Jenn Colella, Idina Menzel, and Mamie Parris

    C. Jenn Colella, Astrid Van Wieren, and Sharon Wheatley

    D. Jenn Colella, Sharon Wheatley, and Kendra Kassenbaum

6. How many touring companies of *Hamilton* are open?

    A. 6

    B. 7

    C. 5

    D. 4

7. Who began playing Jenna in the national tour of *Waitress* on September 28?

    A. Desi Oakley

    B. Christine Dwyer

C. Betsy Wolfe

D. Jessie Mueller

8. Who is playing Cynthia Murphy in the *Dear Evan Hansen* Tour?

   A. Christiane Noll

   B. Jennifer Laura Thompson

   C. Jessica Phillips

   D. Rachel Bay Jones

9. How many productions of *Dear Evan Hansen* are open?

   A. 2

   B. 4

   C. 3

   D. 1

10. Who most recently played The Phantom on the US Tour of *Phantom of the Opera*?

    A. Ben Crawford

    B. Norm Lewis

    C. Quentin Oliver Lee

    D. Ramin Karimloo

MEDIUM:

1. Who most recently played Peter Pan in the company of *Finding Neverland*?

   A. Melanie Moore

B. Melody Rose

C. Alison Williams

D. Cathy Rigby

2. Who most recently played Nick Bottom in the *Something Rotten* National Tour?

    A. Brian d'Arcy James

    B. Rob McClure

    C. Matthew Baker

    D. Christian Borle

3. How many companies of *Beautiful: The Carole King Musica*l are running?

    A. 4

    B. 3

    C. 2

    D. 5

4. Who was playing Carole King and Cynthia Weil on the national tour of *Beautiful* as of 2018?

    A. Sarah Bockel and Alison Whitehurst

    B. Chilina Kennedy and Kate Reinders

    C. Jessie Mueller and Anika Larsen

    D. Jessie Mueller and Abby Mueller

5. Who most recently played the Genie in the *Aladdin* touring company?

    A. James Monroe Iglehart

    B. Michael James Scott

    C. Major Attaway

D. Korie Lee Blossey

6. How many productions of *The Book of Mormon* are running?
  A. 2
  B. 3
  C. 5
  D. 4

7. Which two people from *The Book of Mormon* tour came into the Broadway company as a member of the Ensemble?
  A. Donell James Foreman and Derrick Williams
  B. Kevin Clay and Lewis Cleale
  C. Stephen Ashfield and Derrick Williams
  D. Donell James Foreman and Graham Bowen

8. Who originated the role of Rafiki in the 1st National Tour of *The Lion King*?
  A. Tracie Thoms
  B. Fredi Walker-Browne
  C. Sylvia MacCalla
  D. Haneefah Wood

9. How many companies of *The Lion King* are there?
  A. 5
  B. 6
  C. 7
  D. 8

10. Where did *Spongebob Squarepants* begin their tour?
  A. San Francisco
  B. Boston

C. Las Vegas

D. Miami

HARD:

1. How many performances did Carol Channing play as Dolly?
   A. 5,000
   B. 6,000
   C. 1,000
   D. 7,000

2. Who originated the role of Jenna in the *Waitress* tour?
   A. Christine Dwyer
   B. Desi Oakley
   C. Jessie Mueller
   D. Abby Mueller

3. Who played Eva Peron in the National Tour of *Evita*?
   A. Elena Roger
   B. Patti Lupone
   C. Caroline Bowman
   D. Beth Leavel

4. Which Tony nominee played Marvin on the *Falsettos* tour?
   A. Max Von Essen
   B. Christian Borle
   C. Nick Adams
   D. Nick Blaemire

5. Who from the Broadway company reprised their role in the *Charlie and the Chocolate Factory* tour?

    A. Madeleine Doherty

    B. Brynn Williams

    C. Matt Wood

    D. Kathy Fitzgerald

6. Who played Anna Leonowens on *The King and I* tour?

    A. Kelli O'Hara

    B. Angela Baumgardner

    C. Analisa Leaming

    D. Kristen Hahn

7. How many shows has Jess LeProtto performed in on Broadway?

    A. 8

    B. 9

    C. 7

    D. 4

8. Who did Jess LeProtto play in the tour of *Hello, Dolly!*?

    A. Cornelius Hackl

    B. Barnaby Tucker

    C. Ambrose Kemper

    D. Horace Vandergelder

9. Who played Anya in the *Anastasia* tour?
   A. Christy Altomare
   B. Liz Callaway
   C. Lila Coogan
   D. Tari Kelly

10. Who most recently was Tevye in the tour of *Fiddler on the Roof*?
   A. Danny Burstein
   B. Jesse Weil
   C. Etai Benson
   D. Yehezkel Lazarov

ANSWER KEY

Chapter One: Broadway Theaters

EASY:

1. (A) Lesli Margherita
2. (C) Disney
3. (C) Booth Theatre
4. (A) Majestic
5. (B) On Your Feet
6. (A) Gershwin Theatre
7. (D) Ambassador Theatre
8. (A) Eugene O'Neill Theatre
9. (C) 1776
10. (B) Lyceum Theatre

MEDIUM:

1. (A) Selwyn Theatre
2. (C) 17
3. (B) Marquis Theatre
4. (C) Carrying a blue bottle
5. (B) New Amsterdam Theatre
6. (D) Al Hirschfeld Theatre
7. (A) Gerald Schoenfeld Theatre

8. (A) Bernard B. Jacobs Theatre
9. (B) Majestic
10. (A) Golden Theatre

HARD:

1. (A) Heather Tepe
2. (C) Henry Herts & Hugh Tallant
3. (A) Belasco
4. (C) Circle in the Square
5. (D) Richard Rodgers
6. (B) Henry B. Harris
7. (A) Danton's Death
8. (C) Palace Theatre
9. (D) Cort Theatre
10. (D) New Victory Theatre

Chapter Two: History of the Great White Way

EASY:

1. (A) Hal Prince
2. (C) Chicago
3. (B) The white lights from the Theatre marquis
4. (B) Motion Pictures
5. (C) 500
6. (C) Between 2,000 and 2,500 performances
7. (B) 1943-1959
8. (C) 1776

9. (C) Hair
10. (C) Macbeth

MEDIUM:

1. (B) 41
2. (C) 5.5 Hours
3. (B) A Trip to Chinatown
4. (A) The Lambs
5. (C) Waitress
6. (D) 101
7. (A) Polly Browne
8. (A) Kern & Hammerstein
9. (B) Downtown Manhattan
10. (D) Nine new theatres were built

HARD:

1. (A) 1776
2. (D) Lightnin'
3. (D) 1985
4. (A) The Cradle Will Rock
5. (D) This is the Army
6. (C) 1881
7. (B) May 26th, 1913
8. (C) The chorus member with the most Broadway credits
9. (A) Ghost Light
10. (D) Whistle

Chapter Three: Name That Tune

EASY:

1. (B) Lin Manuel Miranda
2. (A) Fix your hair
3. (C) In The Heights
4. (A) Can You Feel The Love Tonight
5. (C) Hello, Dolly!
6. (C) 2017
7. (B) Andrew Lloyd Webber
8. (B) Wonderful Boy
9. (D) Mamma Mia!
10. (B) "Where is the life that late I led? / Where is it now? Totally dead."

MEDIUM:

1. (D) Be More Chill
2. (A) Sara Bareilles
3. (C) South Pacific
4. (D) I'll Hold Your Hand
5. (A) "A ball and that's not all! / The Prince is giving a ball"
6. (A) 1996
7. (D) Evita
8. (A) I'm Not That Smart
9. (D) Sheldon Harnick
10. (A) Let's Call The Shots

HARD:

1. (A) Pitch the quick fantastic
2. (A) Fred Ebb
3. (B) Savings you accrue together
4. (C) Queen Mab
5. (D) We can handle that
6. (B) Calvin Berger
7. (D) Look At Her
8. (C) 2002
9. (A) Starbuck
10. (D) Brigadoon

Chapter Four: Tony Award Trivia

EASY:

1. (C) Julie Taymor
2. (C) Hamilton
3. (C) Audra McDonald
4. (B) Thoroughly Modern Millie
5. (A) Gypsy
6. (B) My Fair Lady
7. (C) Into the Woods
8. (C) Avenue Q
9. (C) Antoinette Perry
10. (A) Dear Evan Hansen

MEDIUM:

1. (D) Scottsboro Boys
2. (D) Nathan Lane
3. (D) Aaron Tveit
4. (A) Cicely Tyson
5. (C) The Apple Tree
6. (C) Kiss Me, Kate
7. (A) Mister Roberts
8. (B) 1947
9. (D) The Producers
10. (A) Redhead

HARD:

1. (A) Camelot
2. (B) Julie Andrews
3. (D) Frankie Michaels
4. (D) Brock Pemberton
5. (C) Waldorf Astoria, New York
6. (A) Fiorello!
7. (A) 1963
8. (B) 2012
9. (A) 1974
10. (B) Death of a Salesman

(cont.)

Chapter Five: Writers and Composers

EASY:

1. (A) Pal Joey
2. (B) The Sound of Music
3. (C) The Lion King
4. (D) Sara Bareilles
5. (D) Fall Out Boy
6. (A) Kinky Boots
7. (B) Porgy & Bess
8. (D) Minchin & Miranda
9. (A) Oscar Hammerstein
10. (A) Fun Home

MEDIUM:

1. (D) How to Succeed in Business Without Really Trying
2. (C) "If I Loved You"
3. (A) The Likes Of Us
4. (B) Chess
5. (B) Singin' In the Rain
6. (D) Golden Gate
7. (B) Jeanine Tesori
8. (B) March 22nd
9. (C) The Shot Heard Round the World
10. (A) Sacrimmoralinority

1. (B) Rodgers and Hart
2. (B) 1992
3. (C) Jule Styne
4. (D) Venice
5. (A) 37th Academy Awards
6. (D) Shrek 2
7. (C) Lorenz Hart
8. (A) 1985
9. (A) Charles Strouse
10. (B) Stephen Schwartz

Chapter Six: Broadway's Brightest Stars

EASY:

1. (C) Ethel Merman
2. (C) Kerstin Anderson
3. (A) Phillipa Soo
4. (B) Carole King
5. (C) Wicked
6. (A) Idina Menzel
7. (A) Jean Valjean
8. (D) Nathan Lane
9. (C) Newsies
10. (B) Audra McDonald

MEDIUM:

1. (A) Sweeney Todd
2. (A) Taye Diggs
3. (B) 5
4. (B) Sherie Rene Scott
5. (C) Bette Midler
6. (B) Nic Rouleau
7. (A) Christian Borle
8. (C) Jessie Mueller
9. (B) 12
10. (A) 6

HARD:

1. (B) Chita Rivera
2. (A) Patti Ann LuPone
3. (C) Christina Applegate
4. (A) 4
5. (B) Jake Epstein, Jason Gotay, Matt Caplan, and Matthew Wilkas
6. (D) Ryan McCartan
7. (B) Dax Shepard
8. (A) Leona Lewis
9. (C) Samantha Barks
10. (C) 6

(cont.)

Chapter Seven: Famous Flops

EASY:

1. (B) Mitch Leigh
2. (C) $8 Million
3. (A) All About Me
4. (D) Amelie
5. (B) Dave Thomas Brown
6. (D) New Century Theatre
7. (C) 2007
8. (D) 36 Performances
9. (A) State Fair
10. (C) Carrie

MEDIUM:

1. (B) Carnival in Flanders
2. (C) Candide
3. (A) Breakfast at Tiffany's
4. (B) The Rocky Horror Picture Show
5. (A) Taboo
6. (B) Cyrano
7. (D) Christopher Walken
8. (A) 40
9. (B) Does a Tiger Wear a Necktie?
10. (C) My Favorite Year

1. (A) Liza's at the Palace
2. (C) Slapstick Tragedy
3. (C) The Life and Adventures of Nicholas Nickleby
4. (A) All my Sons
5. (D) Passion
6. (A) Spiderman: Turn Off the Dark
7. (B) Kelly
8. (A) Via Galactica
9. (C) M. Butterly
10. (A) Big Fish

Chapter Eight: Holiday Hits

EASY:

1. (B) White Christmas
2. (C) Holiday Inn
3. (B) Turkey Lurkey Time
4. (B) Annie
5. (C) Meet Me in St. Louis
6. (B) Hanukkah or Chanukkah
7. (B) She Loves Me
8. (B) Singing it loud for all to hear
9. (C) Ebenizer Scrooge - A Christmas Carol
10. (B) How the Grinch Stole Christmas

MEDIUM:

1. (A) Billy Elliot
2. (D) 6
3. (A) Christmas and New Years Eve
4. (B) Mame
5. (A) A Christmas Story
6. (B) The Grinch
7. (A) Sebastian Arcelus & George Wendt
8. (C) Lesli Margherita
9. (B) It's a Wonderful Life
10. (A) November 14, 2010 - January 2, 2011

HARD:

1. (D) Alvin and the Chipmunks
2. (D) Daisy Eagan
3. (A) Ali Ewoldt
4. (C) 4
5. (B) Rachel Bay Jones
6. (C) Eddie Korbich
7. (A) Molly Shannon
8. (B) Jane Lynch
9. (A) 6
10. (C) John Truitt

(cont.)

Chapter Nine: National Tours

EASY:

1. (A) Betty Buckley
2. (B) 8
3. (D) 4
4. (A) 5
5. (A) Jenn Colella, Rachel Tucker, and Becky Gulsvig
6. (C) 5
7. (B) Christine Dwyer
8. (A) Chrisiane Noll
9. (C) 3
10. (C) Quentin Oliver Lee

MEDIUM:

1. (B) Melody Rose
2. (C) Matthew Baker
3. (A) 4
4. (A) Sarah Bockel & Alison Whitehurst
5. (B) Michael James Scott
6. (D) 4
7. (A) Donell James Foreman & Derrick Williams
8. (B) Fredi Walker-Browne
9. (D) 8
10. (C) Las Vegas

HARD:

1. (A) 5,000
2. (B) Desi Oakley
3. (C) Caroline Bowman
4. (A) Max Von Essen
5. (D) Kathy Fitzgerald
6. (B) Angela Baumgardner
7. (A) 8
8. (B) Barnaby Tucket
9. (C) Lila Coogan
10. (D) Yehezkel Lazarov